WITH OR WITHOUT YOU

The Prospect for Jews in Today's Russia

ACADEMIC
STUDIES
PRESS

WITH OR WITHOUT YOU

THE PROSPECT FOR JEWS
IN TODAY'S RUSSIA

MAXIM D. SHRAYER

BOSTON
2017

Earlier versions of the Prologue and Chapters 1–5 of this book were published
in *Mosaic Magazine* as its March 2017 essay of the month: https://
mosaicmagazine.com/essay/2017/03/the-prospect-for-russias-jews/

An earlier version of "In Closing" was published in *Tablet Magazine* on March 7,
2017: http://www.tabletmag.com/scroll/226922/is-it-time-to-compose-an-elegy-
for-russias-jewry

All translations from the Russian, unless noted otherwise,
are the author's own.

Library of Congress Cataloging-in-Publication Data

Names: Shrayer, Maxim, 1967- author.

Title: With or without you : the prospect for Jews in today's Russia / Maxim D.
Shrayer.

Description: Boston : Academic Studies Press, [2017] | Series: Jews of Russia &
Eastern Europe and their legacy | Includes bibliographical references and index.

Identifiers: LCCN 2017033363 (print) | LCCN 2017035254 (ebook) | ISBN
9781618116604 (e-book) | ISBN 9781618116598 (paperback)

Subjects: LCSH: Jews—Russia (Federation)—History—21st century. |
Jews—Russia (Federation)—Identity. | Russia (Federation)—Ethnic
relations. | BISAC: HISTORY / Europe / Russia & the Former Soviet Union. |
RELIGION / Religion, Politics & State.

Classification: LCC DS134.86 (ebook) | LCC DS134.86 .S57 2017 (print) | DDC
305.892/4047--dc23

LC record available at https://lccn.loc.gov/2017033363

ISBN 978-1-61811-658-9 (paperback)
ISBN 978-1-61811-660-4 (electronic)

Cover design by Ivan Grave.

On the cover: Moscow cadets at the Jewish Museum and Tolerance Center,
photograph from the website of the Department of Multicultural Policy,
Interregional Cooperation and Tourism of Moscow,
http://welcome.mos.ru/presscenter/news/detail/5701905.html

Published by Academic Studies Press in 2017

28 Montfern Avenue
Brighton, MA 02135, USA
press@academicstudiespress.com
www.academicstudiespress.com

To Emilia Shrayer
and David Shrayer-Petrov,
with love

Contents

Prologue: "G-d Gave Me as a Jew Such a Place in Life"

"Why do you stay here?"

"I have a son here," Oleg Dorman replied with an intonation redolent of Pasternak's long poem *Spektorsky*, which my father used to read to me when I was in high school. And then Dorman added, "G-d gave me as a Jew such a place in life—to live in Russia."

"What about the other Jews? Why do they stay here?"

"About the others I don't know, but I imagine they too are needed here by Nature and the Creator."

Dorman and I seem always to be having the same conversation about Russian Jews: staying or leaving? He stayed; I, a child of refuseniks—Soviet Jews denied permission to emigrate—spent the first twenty years of my life in Moscow before leaving in 1987. For his son, born in the 2000s, Dorman chose the name "David," and in Russia such a name marks one forever as a non-Russian—most likely a Jew, a Georgian, or an Armenian. Every time, on one or another of my periodic visits to the city, talking with Dorman is like a session of acupuncture, except that instead of relief it produces fresh pain. Our latest round took place in late October and early November of 2016. It began after a lecture I'd just given at the Jewish Museum and Tolerance Center on October 30, 2016, and continued the next day in the lobby of a grand Moscow hotel over tea and biscuits with apricot jam.

I've known Dorman, a second-generation filmmaker, for many years. Most of his films treat Jewish-Russian

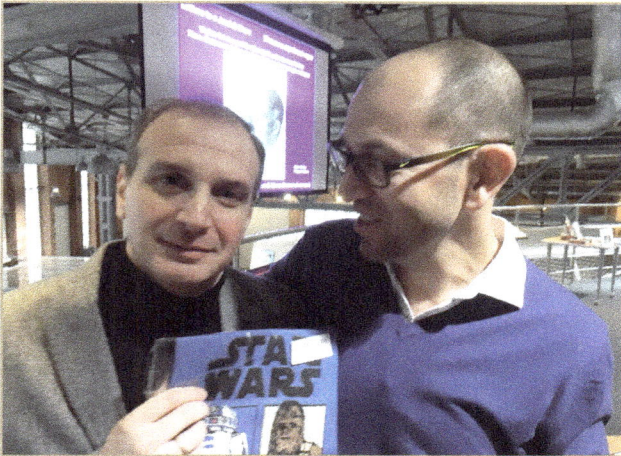

Oleg Dorman and Maxim D. Shrayer.
Moscow, October 30, 2016. Photo by Maxim Mussel.

subjects, notably *Desire to Know* (1995), which tells the story of Yeshiva Torat Chaim, founded in 1989 by Rabbi Moshe Soloveitchik of Zurich on the site of a former Communist-party "vacation home" southwest of Moscow. In 2009 Dorman gained national acclaim after the release of *Word for Word*, his celebrated documentary about Lilianna Lungina, the esteemed Jewish-Russian literary translator. More recently, Dorman, who is also Woody Allen's Russian translator, has been translating the work of Paul Gallico, the American novelist and sportswriter. Author of *The White Goose* and *Verna*, the half-Italian, half-Austrian Gallico is probably best remembered today for his comment on Jewish basketball players: "The reason, I suspect, that basketball appeals to the Hebrew with his Oriental background, is that the game places a premium on an alert, scheming mind, flashy trickiness, artful dodging and general smart aleckness."

An agemate of mine, Dorman dresses in wool slacks and cardigans and looks like a slightly Jewish version of one of Chekhov's intellectuals, aggrieved by the public's lack of aesthetic refinement. As we talked, we were sipping buckthorn tea and noshing on tiny ornate biscuits. My fifth-grade daughter Mira, who had accompanied me to Russia, was absorbed in my smartphone.

"Did you know," asked Dorman, "that when the tram approaches the stop for the museum, they announce it as 'Museum and Tolerance Center' and not 'Jewish Museum and Tolerance Center?'"

"No way! Not possible."

"Well, all you need to do is go there. By tram. Not by cab."

"Do you think they drop the word deliberately?"

"Drop or forget, I don't know," Dorman replied. "But I think it's absurd. No less than absurd. They announce it as 'Museum and Tolerance Center.' What museum? Museum of what?"

I was in Moscow for five days. I had to go see for myself.

1. A Visit to the Museum

Jewish Museum and Tolerance Center. Moscow, October 30, 2016.
Photo by Maxim D. Shrayer.

If you should ever find yourself in Moscow and want to understand how things go with Russia's Jews, visit the Jewish Museum and Tolerance Center in the neighborhood of Maryina Roshcha (Mary's Grove), located a few miles north of Moscow's historic center. The museum, which opened in 2012, just six years ago, occupies a section of what in the post-Soviet decades has emerged as the spinal cord of Jewish communal, religious, and cultural life in Russia's capital: a whole campus with a synagogue, a community center, educational institutions, a publishing house, a bookstore, and medical offices.

It takes many hours to tour the museum's permanent exhibits, but as a foreign tourist with only a couple of hours to spare between a planned excursion to Red Square and a ballet performance at the Bolshoi, you might wish to bypass the earliest galleries and glide instead through the halls reconstructing life in the shtetl, then whisper a prayer in the re-created sanctuary of a wooden synagogue from Ukraine, and stand for a few minutes in the gallery dedicated to the Russian Revolution and civil war. Just make sure you give yourself enough time for Gallery 8, "Soviet Union: 1922–1941." Here is unique stuff, not to be found in any Jewish museum outside of Russia, dedicated to the two all-important decades of early Soviet history and the myriad contributions that Jews made to Soviet civilization. Then, after briefly setting foot in the semicircular Gallery 9, "Holocaust and the Great Patriotic War" (featuring a war plane and a tank like the ones flown or driven into battle by Jewish heroes of the Soviet Union) and lingering a bit in Gallery 12, "Perestroika to the Present," you can head for refreshment to the museum's lovely kosher café called Aleph.

The talk I gave at the museum, preceding my conversation with Oleg Dorman, was titled "Letters to a Jewish Muse" and took place in the building's jazzy education center. In the talk I explored the marriage of Vladimir Nabokov and Véra Slonim, a Jewish woman who never converted to Christianity. Questions from the audience focused on mixed marriages and antisemitism. A Jewish man in his fifties, dressed in a lustrous double-breasted suit, got up from the front row, face blotchy with nervousness. Almost choking, he said that not only did every Russian have an antisemite buried deep inside his or her heart but every Jew, too, harbored his or her own secret self-hater. The gentleman turned out to be the Moscow representative of a major American corporation. As he delivered his tirade, I thought I'd stumbled into a Russian version of an Arthur Miller play about an over-the-top family feud.

"Who were the people in the audience?" I later asked Liya Chechik, director of the museum's public programs. Although she didn't have specific demographic data, she ventured that the attendees would have included "Moscow Jews steeped in the Jewish cultural life of the capital and people who have nothing whatsoever to do with Jewishness." And this was precisely the mixed audience the museum wanted to attract, she added: "people of different backgrounds [who] will come here and not be afraid of the word 'Jewish' in the name and at the same time Jews [who] will always find something interesting for themselves."

1. A Visit to the Museum

To me, who grew up a refusenik, the very existence of an institution such as Moscow's Jewish Museum and Tolerance Center seems more unreal than the existence of "fantastic beasts" (as in the movie of that name about a secret New York society of witches and wizards) does to my American-born children. Like other such museums, including Warsaw's POLIN, Berlin's Jüdisches Museum, and Philadelphia's American Jewish History Museum, the Moscow museum negotiates between telling a story of Jews and telling a Jewish story—the two stories being the contrasting and competing accounts of Jewish vs. Russian/Soviet triumphs and tribulations. The museum serves as a post-Soviet model of how the centripetal forces of Jewish

"Jews become an integral part of Soviet society."
Gallery 8, Jewish Museum and Tolerance Center.
Photo by Maxim D. Shrayer.

universalism counteract the centrifugal forces of Jewish exceptionalism in today's Russian context.

Is this the best Jewish museum one could expect in an authoritarian, postcolonial nation with trappings of cultural and religious pluralism and a looming threat of further political retrenchment? I think the answer is yes, but a recent polemic in the pages of the journal *East European Jewish Affairs* threw into relief some diverging views of the museum's mission in today's Russia. The occasion was a skeptical review of the museum by Olga Gershenson, a professor at the University of Massachusetts who was born in the former USSR and immigrated to the United States by way of Israel.

According to Gershenson, the museum "asserts that Jews are part and parcel of the Russian nation, and their triumphal story makes them a model Russian minority." Finding this way of portraying historical reality rather suspect, she elucidates it by pointing to the "close ties between the Chabad-Lubavitch leadership and Putin's regime, as well as Putin's well-publicized support" for [establishing] the museum—factors that in her view "created the perception that the museum-in-the-making would be an officially sanctioned institution, even though it was created with private funds."

The notion of Russia's Jews as a "model," or exemplary minority, ruffled the feathers of some of the museum's creators. Two letters were appended to Gershenson's review in *East European Jewish Affairs*, both from historians who had served on the Content Committee tasked by the Federation of Jewish Communities of Russia with developing the museum's exhibition. The Moscow-based historian Oleg Budnitsky dismissed charges of an official political agenda and attacked Gershenson for portraying the museum as a vehicle of a "Kremlin-Chabad conspiracy" [Budnitsky's formula, not Gershenson's] . . . "to represent the Jews . . . as Russia's 'model minority.'" In justifying the story told by the museum, Budnitsky added:

> Soviet Jews in the late 1930s and early 1940s were not the "Jews of silence" [the title of Elie Wiesel's 1966 book on the condition of Soviet Jews]. They constituted the most successful Soviet nation; Jews were on the whole the most Soviet of all Soviet people. They were the most educated and most overrepresented among the highest-prestige professions, in the Soviet and party apparatus. . . . They considered themselves above all to be Soviet people, and only after that as Jews.

Indeed, in "Soviet Union, 1922–1941"—the gallery of the Jewish Museum and Tolerance Center where I've urged you to spend time—one section is titled "Jews Become an Integral Part of Soviet Society." Here a visitor would learn that by the 1930s Jews were seen by all as "exemplary evidence of Soviet success."

Poster of Maxim D. Shrayer's lecture at the Jewish Museum and Tolerance Center. "Letters to a Jewish Muse: The Life of Vladimir Nabokov and Véra Slonim as Literature and History." Moscow, October 30, 2016. (Véra and Vladimir Nabokov, 1934, Berlin, photo by Nicholas Nabokov.)

There is some truth to this statement, as there is to Budnitsky's forceful words intended to reaffirm it. Yet its employment in a Jewish museum in Russia gives me goose bumps. Paraphrasing a well-known joke, the historian John D. Klier remarked, "Soviet rule up to 1945 may be characterized as 'good for the Jew, but bad for the Jews.'" As defenses go, Budnitsky's might have been more persuasive if it had also acknowledged the flipside of Jewish survival and advancement in the Soviet Union: the regime's efforts in those same decades to annihilate Judaism and traditional Jewish life.

Not that the efforts completely succeeded. In the 1920s, my four grandparents moved from the former Pale of Settlement to earn workers' status and attend universities in great Soviet cities. They enjoyed professional success and upward mobility, but they most certainly didn't believe that Jews were "the most Soviet of all Soviet people." Nor did they ever shed the native skin of their Jewishness. Every Friday, my paternal grandmother Bella, the daughter of a Litvak rabbi who would be murdered in his own home in the summer of 1941, cooked gefilte fish and noodle kugel in a communal apartment on Leningrad's working-class Vyborg Side. As for my maternal grandfather, Aron (Arkady), throughout his life, which ended in Moscow in 1975, he never gave up hope of being allowed to see Israel and reunite with siblings who had emigrated to the Mandate of Palestine in the early 1920s. I doubt I'm the only Soviet Jew born in the 1960s who would demur if his or her grandparents were touted as evidence of Jewish-Soviet success.

All in all, the museum's galleries flood me with mixed emotions. I feel a measure of pride over the Jewish contributions to Soviet culture and society. I also feel deep sorrow. But, above all, I feel a dearth of connection with the aspirations of *today's* Russian Jews. My reaction stems in part from an exile's sense of displacement. I take pleasure in immersing myself in the history of Jews in the Slavic lands, and I enjoy bringing my children to this Jewish museum—if "enjoy" is the right word for what feels a bit like visiting the graves of our ancestors in the Preobrazhenskoe Jewish Cemetery on the outskirts of St. Petersburg. The graves are ours, and, in the museum's later galleries, the faces of refuseniks are also ours. But the story of Jews in today's Russia is no longer our story. Who are the real heirs-designate of the Jews of the early Soviet decades? Is the Jewish Museum and Tolerance Center a museum of those who stayed in Russia or of those, by far the majority, who would leave as soon as they could?

In 1989, according to the last official Soviet census, there were 1,480,000 Jews in the USSR, of whom 570,500 were living in the Russian Soviet Federative Republic. Data recently synthesized by Mark Tolts of the Hebrew University, a leading demographer of Jews in post-Soviet space, put the 2016 number of Jews in the Russian Federation at about 180,000, a bit over one-tenth the size of the 1989 figure. (Of the 180,000, about 61,000 resided in Moscow and about 27,000 in St. Petersburg.) Even if we account for the fact that the 1989 statistic includes hundreds of thousands of Jews in Ukraine and other places not part of today's Russian Federation, the numbers tell a story of drastic attrition.

In Isaac Babel's story "How It Was Done in Odessa," the gangster Benya Krik, echoing the words of Sholem Aleichem's Tevye the Dairyman, intones:

> But wasn't it a mistake on G-d's part to settle Jews in Russia, where they would be tortured like in hell? And would it be so bad if Jews lived in Switzerland, where first-class lakes, mountain air,

and Frenchmen surrounded them everywhere? Everybody makes mistakes, even G-d.

If settling Jews in Russia was one of G-d's mistakes, G-d can also correct such mistakes. The trajectory of Jewish-Russian history over the past 30 years suggests a large-scale correction. I go around Moscow, which used to be my home, and I reflect on Babel's words and on the future of Russia's dwindling Jewish community.

2. A Streetcar Named Oblivion

Streetcars are stubborn animals. Relics of a long-gone past, they insist on outliving their time. For myself, having overdosed on them in my Soviet youth, I usually avoid both streetcars and buses in my visits to Moscow. For fast connections there's always the metro, but in general I prefer to walk or else to take cabs, now almost as omnipresent as they are in Manhattan and relatively inexpensive.

Yet here I was on November 1, 2016, taking Moscow tram No. 19 for a return visit to the Jewish Museum and Tolerance Center. Tram No. 19 had originally been launched in 1912; its route was revised in the victorious 1945 and shut down in 1950. Following Stalin's death, it was relaunched as a new route and then expanded and revamped three times since the collapse of the Soviet Union in 1991. The route of tram No. 19 forms a lopsided boot the shape of Italy flipped around and then turned 90 degrees clockwise. It was about one in the afternoon. The run, which takes about 30 minutes, links the area of the Three Stations, Moscow's biggest railway hub, with the Novoslobodskaya metro stop just north of the center. A large portion of the route traverses Moscow's

Moscow Tram No. 19 en route to the Jewish Museum and Tolerance Center. November 1, 2016. Photo by Maxim D. Shrayer.

neighborhood of Mary's Grove, a historic area of Jewish life in old Moscow and, as I've mentioned, a hotbed of Jewish religious and communal life in today's Russia. Jewish tradesmen and working poor settled here and in Moscow's other northeastern and northern suburbs in the last decades of the nineteenth century, when a residence permit was officially required. In ramshackle cottages and tool sheds, these transplants from the Pale of Settlement could lie low and escape police surveillance, awaiting a change in Jewish fortunes.

In 1926, defying historical odds, a wooden synagogue was erected in Mary's Grove just as synagogues across the USSR were being closed down and turned into storage spaces or temples of atheist propaganda. The wooden synagogue burned down in 1993, and the Moscow Jewish Community Center rose in its place, to open in 2000 under the auspices of Chabad-Lubavitch. In 1926 a city bus depot had been built nearby, a Constructivist edifice that would eventually be transformed into the Jewish Museum and Tolerance Center. Mary's Grove is not only an area of Moscow rife with Jewish history but also one linked with the criminal underworld. Recent Russian TV shoot-'em-ups about incorruptible Soviet cops fighting vice in the 1940s and early 1950s picture Mary's Grove as a fiefdom of wooden houses, chicken coops, overgrown gardens, devout Jews in yarmolkes, and frisky gangsters with gold teeth.

To visualize the area surrounding the Jewish Museum and Tolerance Center, one needs to look at a map of Moscow, find Red Square, and move one's gaze directly north. Once you've covered the distance of about 7 miles, you're in the middle of Mary's Grove. The area's northwest boundary is Savelovsky railroad station, a fulcrum of suburban trains. Another landmark of the area's northwest extremity is Butyrskaya Prison, or Butyrka, one of the oldest in Russia and Moscow's largest. Rebels against the tsar and political prisoners were kept here in solitary confinement. Houdini performed here in 1908 and freed himself from chains and the "transportation box" in all of 28 minutes. In 1937–38, during the Great Terror, some 20,000 inmates were simultaneously held in Butyrka. Among the prison's famous literary inmates were Osip Mandelstam and Evgenia Ginzburg. Refusenik activists were kept here during interrogation and inquest, among them the prisoner of Zion Viktor Brailovsky, a man of great courage, nobleness and charisma, whom I had the pleasure of meeting at a refusenik gathering I attended with my parents in 1986—soon after Brailovsky's release from the gulag. North of Mary's Grove are factories and service tracks, beyond them to the north—some of the city's shabbiest former suburbs and working-class settlements.

When I was coming of age in Moscow in the 1970s, I identified Mary's Grove with lingering squalor, relative inaccessibility by metro, and three more things. One was the building of the former Mariinsky Hospital for the Poor, where Fyodor Dostoevsky's father served as a staff physician and where Dostoevsky himself was born and spent much of his first fifteen years. Another was the Theater of the Soviet Army, one of Moscow's worst despite its architectural grandeur. A third was what many refuseniks called the "Hasidic shul"—this, in contrast to the historic Moscow Choral Synagogue in the city center (the main locus of Orthodox Judaism in Russia). Back in Soviet days, when one paid a price for being unabashedly Jewish, the street outside the Moscow Choral Synagogue was also a place for displaying Jewish pride.

Boarding tram No. 19, I paid and asked, "How many stops to the Jewish Museum?" The driver, who looked as if he'd recently moved to Moscow from some place one wouldn't want to be alone at night, sized me up and answered, "How do I know?"

"You're the driver," I said.

At this point a sinewy man in his sixties, dressed in a black shearling jacket, stepped forward and said, "Three."

I pulled out my phone and prepared to record the announcement. Students were clustered near the middle doors of the car. The tram made one stop, then another, and as the newcomers pushed their way inside and the tram pulled off and gathered speed, a wheezy announcement rang out: "Next stop—Palace of Culture of MIIT, Museum and Center of Tolerance."

So Oleg Dorman had been right.

As for "MIIT," the acronym refers to the Institute of Railroad Engineering, founded in 1896 as the Moscow Imperial College of the Department of Railroad Transportation. Since 2015 the engineering school has been officially renamed as the Moscow Emperor Nicholas II State University of Railroad Transportation, but in public memory the old name still endures.

For Jews of my vintage, MIIT epitomized the predicament of Jewish college applicants. In the Soviet 1960s–1980s, unwritten quotas made it difficult for Jews to gain admission to many top-tier universities, especially in the humanities and social sciences but also in medicine and hard science. As a result, some engineering schools, where the de-facto Jewish quota was less restrictive, became ghettos of Jewish higher learning. In Moscow, MIIT, as well as the Gubkin Institute of Oil and Gas and the Kosygin Textile Institute, belonged in this category. I remember the advice given to Jewish college applicants in the form of a translingual ditty: *Esli ty a id, postupai v MIIT,/ esli goy, postypai v drugoy*, in which the Yiddish *a id* (a Jew) rhymes with the acronym MIIT whereas *goy* rhymes with the Russian word for "other" or "another." Literally, "If you're a Jew, apply to MIIT,/ If a gentile, apply elsewhere"—that is, to a better and more prestigious university. Or, if one prefers: "If you're a Jew, this school's [MIIT] for you."

In sum, the MIIT tram stop was already loaded with the baggage of Soviet antisemitism. After the founding of the Jewish Museum and Tolerance Center in 2012, the name of the stop was expanded and, one might say, overloaded.

I got off and photographed the sign, attached to a utility pole. It referred only to the railroad engineering school with no mention of the museum. Surrounded by students, I walked up and down Obraztsova Street, then approached the museum's entrance, which was marked by a silvery gray spear-top fence and was accessible through a security checkpoint. As I headed back in the direction of the nearest metro station, I came upon a bus stop for city bus No. 0. The standard black and white sign read, "Palace of Culture 'MIIT'—Museum and Center of Tolerance." Again

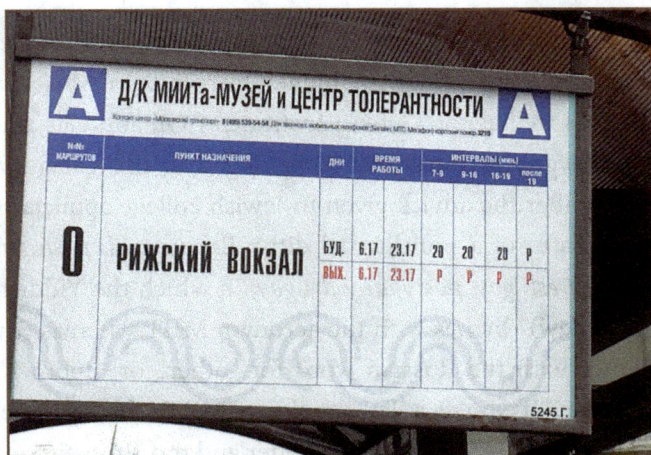

Moscow Bus No. 0. Stop "House of Culture MIIT—Museum and Center of Tolerance. " The word "Jewish" is missing from the name of the stop. November 1, 2016. Photo by Maxim D. Shrayer.

the adjective "Jewish" was missing: deleted, misplaced, obliviated. If you didn't already know where you were, the Jewish character of this museum would have been entirely lost on you.

Various explanations were running through my head, having to do with residual semiotic prejudice, contemporary Russian politics, and basic security concerns. No matter, the absence of the qualifier made for bewilderment and despondency, as though someone had edited the word "Jewish" from the public announcement and whitewashed it on the tram and bus stop signs. This time I didn't go into the museum. On the way to the metro, I stopped at a regular neighborhood supermarket to buy sweets from my Soviet childhood. Along with the nostalgic chocolates and pressed fruit paste I picked up two bottles of Zhuravli ("Cranes"), an "ecologically pure" vodka I like to bring home from my Russia trips.

That evening I Skyped my parents in Boston and told them about my tram ride to the museum and the missing identifier. As teenagers in Moscow and Leningrad, my parents, Emilia Shrayer and David Shrayer-Petrov, had endured the darkest years of Soviet Jewry, when Stalin's wild genocidal paranoia flared until his death in 1953. Both of my parents had lived in Russia for much longer than I would; both are word-workers, sensitive to tone and misuse of language. I wanted to check with them first.

"It's subtle," said my mother, a translator. "In English, Jewish Museum doesn't sound funny." "But in Russian," added my father, a doctor-writer, "*evreiskii muzei* might come across as a bit strange, as though *evreiskii* (Jewish) isn't an obvious attributive, meaning a museum of Jews, but something else, something to be sneered at."

"Oh come on, papa, we're in the year 2016," I retorted. "Things have changed."

"Yes, for some people, maybe. But many people in Russia still think the word 'Jew,' especially the adjective 'Jewish,' is somehow indecent. Not to be said out loud."

"But you said it out loud many times when we lived in Moscow. Openly. In public. In your poetry: 'My Slavic soul in a Jewish wrapping. . . .'"

"That was different. I did it to challenge public perception, to protest antisemitism. And I couldn't publish those poems there," my father replied. "One of the reasons we left."

That was on November 1, 2016, and the next morning I brought up the topic with Boruch Gorin, at forty-five one of the best-known public faces of Russia's Jewish community. As a young Odessan Jew, Gorin answered the call of the late Lubavitcher Rebbe and joined the rebuilders of Jewish life in post-Soviet Russia. Gorin now heads the department of public affairs of the Federation of Jewish Communities of Russia. He also runs the press service of Berel Lazar, who stands at the helm of the Chabad-Lubavitch movement in the Russian Federation (and whom we'll meet soon).

Gorin is the founder and editor-in-chief of *Lekhaim*, a monthly review of culture and politics. Besides the magazine, he also directs the publishing house Knizhniki, renowned for its Russian translations of exemplary modern Jewish fiction and nonfiction, from Bernard Malamud to Philip Roth, from Aharon Appelfeld to Imre Kertész. (I've contributed to both the magazine and the publishing house.) Gorin often publicly addresses sensitive topics, be it a charge of antisemitic activity in a provincial city in the north, a prejudice-oozing comment by a member of the Duma, or a case of Russian figure skaters dancing in striped robes with stars of David affixed to their chests. Combining learnedness and street smarts, Gorin radiates a broadly inclusive view of Jewish culture. Elucidating the position of the Jewish Museum

Boruch Gorin speaking at the Moscow International Conference on Combating Antisemitism. November 2, 2016. Photo by Maxim D. Shrayer.

and Tolerance Center in the context of a recent polemic in *East European Jewish Affairs*, Gorin stated, "One of the key objectives of this landmark project was to create conditions conducive to the improvement of relations among Russian citizens who belong to diverse religious and national groups."

Hotel Radisson Royale (formerly Hotel Ukraina).
Moscow, November 1, 2016. Photo by Maxim D. Shrayer.

We had coffee in the lobby of the former Hotel Ukraina, site of an international conference on combating antisemitism that we both attended (and which I'll also return to). "I went back to the Jewish Museum yesterday," I told Gorin. "Did you know that the word 'Jewish' is missing from the tram announcement?"

"Yes," Gorin replied, taking a sip of coffee, his tall brow furrowed.

"What do you make of it?"

Odessan inflections pulsating in his rich and varied Russian speech, Gorin explained that in the popular

Russian imagination, cognates of the word *evrei* ("Jew") and the adjective *evreiskii* ("Jewish") have retained something of a funny flavor. "No longer a dirty word, for sure, but still perhaps suggesting something awkward or pitiful to some members of the Russian public."

I lowered my gaze, gripped by a sudden recollection of a music-appreciation class in my old Moscow school. I think it was in sixth grade, around the winter of 1979–80. Soviet troops were about to invade or had just invaded Afghanistan.

On that day, Mussorgsky's *Pictures at an Exhibition* were in the lesson plan. Would it have been too much for our teacher to explain to the class that the section we were about to hear, titled "Samuel Goldenberg and Shmuyle" in the composer's original score, came to be known in Russian under the name "Two Jews: Rich and Poor"? But no such luck. Ms. Russian Music merely said, "This next piece you're going to hear is called 'Two Jews.' It represents—"

But before she had a chance to continue her explication, before she could go on about Mussorgsky's "class-conscious genius," half of my classmates exploded in ugly laughter. The mere mention of the word "Jew" had sent the boys, and also a few girls, into hysterics. To them it had the ring of a particularly juicy swear word—and now their teacher herself had used it. And there were two whole Jews, as though one weren't enough! Several kids turned to me, the only Jew in our class, slashing me with their eyes. This humiliation, through which I sat frozen, pretending that it didn't affect me personally, went on until the teacher finally clapped her hands to restore order and extinguished the savagely cascading hilarity.

"Is it something like that?" I asked Gorin, having summed up my recollection and hoping he would say no. But Gorin contended that this was a generational matter, bound to disappear in time. As part of his work at the museum's Tolerance Center, he had been developing public programs aimed at preventing xenophobia and prejudice. The new generation of Russian young people, Gorin asserted, was free of such complexes and misconceptions, such "dirt."

My own experience, much less extensive than that of a Jewish community leader, confirms that in the Russian language the adjective "Jewish" may indeed be losing its residual pitifulness or derisiveness. But does this mean that the adjective "Jewish" will eventually be instated in the name of the tram stop? Is Moscow tram No. 19 destined to stop at the *Jewish* Museum and Tolerance Center? About that I'm not so sure.

3. Gauging Russian Antisemitism

Jewish memory works in ways both mysterious and predictable, impalpable and palpable, speedy and inert. I feel this acutely during annual or biannual trips to my former homeland, which I'm always excited to visit and relieved to depart from. This last trip, during which my daughter Mira and I spent five days in Moscow in late October–early November 2016, had been triggered by an invitation to participate in "Protecting the Future: The Moscow International Conference on Combating Antisemitism." The two-day assembly was held under the joint auspices of the Russian Jewish Congress (an umbrella organization roughly equivalent to the UJA-Federation in the United States), the World Jewish Congress, and the city of Moscow. The conference enjoyed the support of Genesis Philanthropy Group, which sees its mission as "develop[ing] and enhanc[ing] a sense of Jewish identity among Russian-speaking Jews worldwide."

The conference program featured two full days of plenary meetings, academic panels, and roundtables, their topics ranging from antisemitism in the media and sports to Jewish-Christian and Jewish-Muslim relations, and from Holocaust denial to tolerance education. Only four of about sixty conference papers touched on aspects of official and popular antisemitism in the Soviet 1970s–1980s and on the great Jewish emigration from the former USSR. Such a low proportion may be indicative of a dearth of attention these topics receive in today's Russian education, culture, and politics. (The Moscow historian Dmitry Shusharin, author of *Russian Totalitarianism: Freedom Here and Now* [2017], observes a growing trend of idealization of Soviet life in today's Russia and, specifically, of silencing the history of antisemitism of the late Soviet decades. And this is Shusharin's poignant explanation of this trend: "The people who are now at the top are the very ones who used to denounce Zionism at Komsomol rallies.") At the conference, I moderated a panel on "Antisemitism and Jewish Identity" and gave a paper on "Antisemitism and the Decline of Russian Village Prose," which some members of the audience received with a notable discomfort.

In between the talks, private meetings, and conference panels, I showed Mira parts of my native city. It was her third trip to Russia, but her first visit to winter-time Moscow. Under the current mayor, Sergey Sobyanin, Moscow's sidewalks had been largely purged of their stalls, kiosks, and small businesses. More a cleansing of the past than an urban cleanup, the mayor's effort had eliminated much of the city's characteristic air of an oriental bazaar. Now Moscow looks more naked in its authoritarian glory,

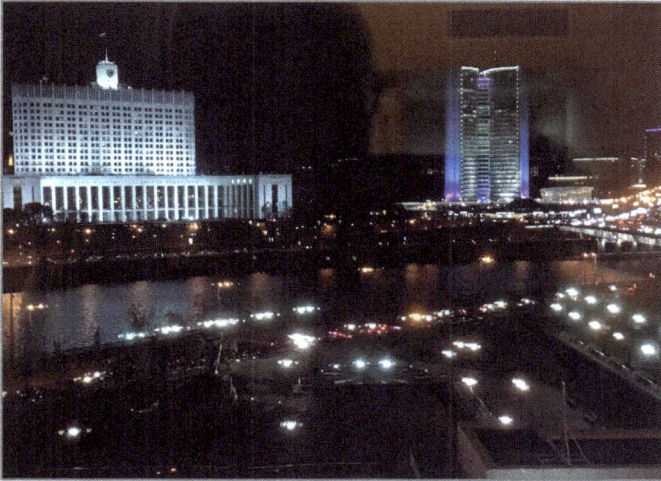

*View of the Moscow River Embankment and the main building
of the Russian government executive (formerly Russian Parliament aka
the "White House"). November 1, 2016. Photo by Maxim D. Shrayer.*

bringing to mind associations with Pinochet's Santiago or
Kim Il-sung's Pyongyang.

Mira and I stayed at the conference hotel, known
to older Muscovites as the Hotel Ukraina but now the
newly refurbished Radisson Royal. It stands on the tip
of an urban peninsula formed by a sinusoid bend of the
Moscow River. In Soviet times this neighborhood, west of
the center and dissected from east to west by Kutuzovsky
Prospect, used to be populated by members of the
party and the government elite. As a kid I considered
Kutuzovsky Prospect a "government route," alien territory,
apparatchik turf. The hotel, which was finished in 1957, is
one of a sisterhood of seven high-rise towers, each of them

a curious spinoff of the Empire State Building and each symbolizing the "empire style" of Stalinist architecture. Bronze statues of Soviet naiads stand in the lobby; original paintings by minor socialist-realist painters crowd the walls.

Our room had a view of the river, beyond which silhouettes of factory chimneys showed gray against the pale Moscow sky. Directly opposite stood the Russian White House, now the main building of the government executive and formerly the seat of the Russian parliament, shelled by army tanks in October 1993 during a standoff between the late President Boris Yeltsin and the parliament. Due to its strategic location, the hotel often hosts diplomats and foreign dignitaries. Plainclothes security men stood in the lobby and conference halls, conversing in hushed tones. At the time of our stay, the hotel also housed a delegation of bodybuilders from Iran; during brief elevator or breakfast encounters, I took a certain stubborn pleasure in discomfiting these mighty Persian men by mentioning that we hailed from Boston.

The conference's opening session on November 1, 2016, attended by an audience of about 200, including a Protestant bishop and a mufti, was an opportunity to observe the outward unanimity with which Russian government officials, leaders of Russia's Jewish community, world Jewish emissaries, and foreign dignitaries all lauded the country's efforts at fighting antisemitism. To my ex-Soviet mind, always skeptical of shared songbooks and choruses of orchestrated praise, this was an extraordinary spectacle. The speakers included Gilad Erdan, Israel's minister of public security and strategic affairs, and Werner Faymann, former chancellor of Austria. Speakers made reference to antisemitism as part and parcel of Russia's long history yet hastened to stress that the country had closed the door on such excrescences. President of the World Jewish Congress Ronald Lauder invoked Russia's "thriving" Jewish community and directly commended its current ruler: "President Putin has made Russia a country where Jews are welcome." In a backward-looking rhetorical leap, Lauder also reminded the audience of the "Russian friends" who had been "on our side": the "brave" Red Army soldiers who fought against Hitlerism and the Russian ambassador who in November 1947 voted "yes" to the UN partition plan for Palestine, which allowed the creation of Israel.

As I listened to the opening speeches, especially those that hearkened back to Nazism and the Shoah, I thought again of parallels with the Soviet 1930s. Back then a Jew felt safer in Moscow than in Berlin, Warsaw, or Budapest, more at ease in Leningrad or Kiev than in London or Paris. But did a Soviet Jew living in a country that appeared to be forgetting how to discriminate against its Jews (I'm paraphrasing a 1939 poem by Yan Satunovsky) also feel less Jewish than Jews living in places of direct danger or daily-enacted prejudice? My mind traveled back to the early Soviet galleries of the Jewish Museum

Mira Isabella Shrayer at the opening of the Moscow International Conference on Combating Antisemitism. November 1, 2016. Photo by Maxim D. Shrayer.

and Tolerance Center. Lost in my train of thought, I was startled by the speech by Ira Forman, former executive director of the National Jewish Democratic Council and then the U.S. special envoy of the Office to Monitor and Combat Antisemitism, a branch of the State Department. Ambassador Forman's remarks echoed the comments by Jewish leaders and other foreign dignitaries. He, too, contrasted antisemitism globally on the rise to its current historical low in Russia today. At the same time, Forman took the position that "antisemitism is not a Jewish problem . . . it's an international problem . . . a human-rights problem." I wondered: Can one monitor a country's level of antisemitism apart from its local context of

Participants of the panel "Antisemitism and Jewish Identity"
at the Moscow International Conference on Combating Antisemitism.
Left to right: Maxim D. Shrayer; Evgenia Lvova; Kirill Feferman;
Stephen Eric Bronner. November 1, 2016.
Photo by Mira Isabella Shrayer.

human-rights violations? Today's Russia may very well be among the world's best places for Jewish living. But can one separate being a Jew from being a thinking subject, a human being of beliefs who suffocates in repressive political conditions?

Perhaps indicative of the relative unimportance of the Jewish question in today's Russian politics was the absence of top Russian officials at the opening ceremonies. Even the mayor of Moscow, an official co-sponsor, sent a deputy to read a bland self-congratulatory statement. The only official who gave a substantive (and eloquent) speech was the jurist Mikhail Fedotov, an adviser to Russia's president and chairman of the Presidential Council for Development of Civic Society and Human Rights. As a young university student in the 1960s, Fedotov had run into difficulties for his connections with the dissident movement, although he later enjoyed a successful career as a law professor. In the view of several otherwise jaundiced colleagues whom I talked to at the conference, Fedotov was one of the "few good people" in the current administration.

Fedotov was at his most provocative when he likened antisemitism to a venereal disease: "like syphilis . . . except that an antisemite isn't ashamed of being an antisemite." But, drawing a pointed contrast, he also invoked the 1993 Russian constitution, which in Article 26 provides that each individual is independently entitled to determine his or her national identification. Paraphrasing and rearranging the order of Paul's famous words in Galatians 3:28, and perhaps not conscious of its polemical context, Fedotov declared, "In the Russian constitution there is neither Greek nor Jew. . . . But, alas"—he was careful enough to concede—"a constitution and life aren't exactly the same thing."

Other opening speeches and subsequent sessions hit the same qualifiedly buoyant note, much as public-health officials welcome a near-eradication of an illness while warning everyone to remain vigilant. In that connection, and for me personally, the intellectual high point was the unveiling, by the sociologist Lev Gudkov and his colleagues at the Levada Center, of their much-anticipated study, "Antisemitism in Today's Russia." An

NGO and one of Russia's largest centers for the study of public opinion, the Levada Center cannot be accused of retailing government positions on the Jewish question and antisemitism in Russia. (In fact, in September 2016 it was placed by Russia's Ministry of Justice on the list of organizations that "perform the functions of a foreign agent.") This was Levada's fourth such study, the earlier ones having been conducted in 1990 (the last Soviet year), 1992, and 1997, thus enabling the authors, in their own words, "to access long-term trends in popular opinions of Jews."

Levada surveyed 1,200 respondents over the age of eighteen and a separate group of 400 residents of Moscow, where the largest number of Russia's Jews resides. Its report examines antisemitism within the larger context of xenophobia and ethnic prejudice and compares opinions about Jews with views of other ethnically defined groups and identities. Although a brief summary cannot do justice to this detailed study, here are some of the main results. Nine percent of those surveyed express "sympathy, interest" toward Jews, while 83 percent hold "no special attitude, just like toward other groups," 6 percent express "resentment, antipathy," and 2 percent register "distrust, fear." The proportion of those holding overtly negative attitudes thus stands at a low 8 percent—as compared with 47 percent holding such views of Roma, 33 percent of Chechens, 25 percent of Arabs, and so forth. In this analysis Jews are in ninth place as targets of antipathy, well below Roma and Tajiks and also below Americans, Ukrainians, and Armenians. When asked, "How would you feel if a Jewish family were your neighbors?" 83 percent responded, "I would have nothing against it," while 56 percent averred they "would have nothing against" their "brother, son, grandson, or another close relative" marrying a Jew.

As compared with previous polls, the report notes, attitudes toward Jews in Russia "have improved dramatically" over the years. Moreover, whereas one of the principal venues of state-sponsored antisemitism in the Soviet Union was official anti-Zionist and anti-Israel propaganda, whose acrid rhetoric clouded the Soviet public's judgment of the Jewish state, the new Levada Center report affirms that "the attitude toward Israel during the last fifteen years has generally remained friendly, neutral, calm."

All this sounds about right to me. Over many years now, during regular visits to Russia, I, too, have observed a decline in overtly antisemitic behavior. During the post-Soviet decades, Jewish stereotypes, no longer propped up by state-sponsored antisemitism, have become more positive. I'm not sure I would go so far as to suggest, as do the authors of this study, that "the dominant attitude toward Jews is that of moderate respect, which is probably a sign that negative connotations are largely gone." But my own experience—granted, as a foreign observer and an American Jew of Russian origin—corroborates the view that Jews are no longer the official number-one enemy of the Russian public, and that, as the Levada report puts it, antisemitism thus holds a fairly insignificant place in the "complex of Russian xenophobic views and ideas" and "may even be called marginal."

Be this as it may, the report also doesn't fail to sound a note of warning. True, the authors write, "the intensity of antisemitic sentiment in Russian society can be considered low and declining. Yet, in some groups antisemitism is not just holding steady but actually expanding."

So what about this oddly counterintuitive finding? The report points to two socioeconomic groups among whom evidence of "actually expanding antisemitism" is to be found: "on the one hand, the 'social periphery' (elderly, poorly educated, low-income)" and—very much on the other hand—among Muscovites who are on average "more educated, well-off, and socially adapted." I was struck by the report's careful negotiation of this picture and by the way the authors envisaged the theoretical emergence of an altogether less rosy scenario: "while admitting the general tendency of decline in antisemitism in Russia, we have to reiterate that it does not render its future rise impossible."

It is a commonly held view that the traditional, ethnic, stereotypical antisemitism is much less prevalent in the Russian mainstream. A Moscow-based Facebook acquaintance of mine, an ethnic Russian who works in IT, explained the low level of public antisemitic behaviors

Cakes "Wise Jew" and "Poor Jew" displayed in Russian supermarkets. 2016. Photos courtesy of Boris Lanin.

by using two terms, *nelikvidno* (literally, "not generating liquidity," meaning "antisemitic behaviors do not produce marketable goods or assets") and *nemodno* ("not fashionable'"). Boris Lanin, a Moscow-based literature professor, whom you will get to know in the pages to follow, sent me two photographs taken at a supermarket patisserie counter in a provincial Russian city. The first photograph features a round chocolate cake, its top decorated with three yellow flowers. I gasped as I read the label: "Cake 'Poor Jew.'" Then I opened the second photograph, this one of a layered chocolate and mousse cake, and marveled at the humor of the label: "Wise Jew." Two cakes, two Jews— in a Russian supermarket. Is this supposed to offend? To hint, subtly, at Mussorgsky's *Pictures at an Exhibition*? To amuse? To attract customers?

Might an implicit or suppressed bias suddenly implode into a new explicit hatred?

During the most recent trip, my daughter and I, both of us foreign and Jewish-looking, visited many public places—museums, parks, the zoo, shopping malls, eateries. We took cabs and the metro and walked about the city. And I didn't hide the fact that I'm a Jew and an expatriate and that Moscow used to be my home. I'll share one encounter. I took Mira to Muzeon Park of Arts, an open-air art and memory space on the bank of the Moscow River about half a mile north of Gorky Park. Alongside contemporary sculptures and installations, which resemble the sculpture garden at the Hirshhorn, Muzeon

Mira Isabella Shrayer with statues of Lenin at Muzeon Park of Arts.
Moscow, October 29, 2016. Photo by Maxim D. Shrayer.

houses Soviet-era statues removed from their previous homes and lumped together on a curated trash heap of Soviet history. There are several Lenins and Brezhnevs and even a granite Stalin with a broken face. Mira and I were standing at the foot of a stately Gorky in an unbuttoned long coat of greening bronze. Gorky had taken off his

*Maxim D. Shrayer and Mira Isabella Shrayer at Muzeon Park of Arts.
(In the background, a Soviet-era installation,*
USSR Is the Foundation of Peace.) *Moscow, October 29, 2016.*

fedora and was about to make a step in the direction of a much taller Dzerzhinsky, "the iron Felix," Polish nobleman and founder of the Soviet secret police. A family of Russian tourists, a man and woman in their early thirties and a girl of about seven, approached us and asked, pointing to the statue moved here with its granite pedestal:

"Do you know who that is?"

"That's Dzerzhinsky," I replied. "It used to stand in Lubyanka Square. Across from Detsky Mir, the children's department store."

All three visitors were dressed in colorful down jackets, and they had no idea I was a foreigner.

"Where else have you been in Moscow?" I asked, mustering up my best Moscow drawl.

"Red Square, the circus . . . ," the woman replied, a bit shyly. "It's our first time."

And then, completely on the spur of the moment, I asked the visitors to Moscow, "Have you been to the Jewish Museum?"

What had come over me? I guess I was interested in seeing how they would respond. "No, where's that?" the man queried, unperturbed.

"It's a great museum," I said and explained how to get there by metro.

Only once during my recent trip, in the course of a reading I gave at Biblio-Globus, one of Moscow's oldest bookstores, did something of an antisemitic incident, laced with anti-Americanism, unravel in my presence. A woman in her seventies, clearly formed during the Soviet years, looking almost like a *New Yorker* caricature of her type, rose during the Q&A and referred to my first having left "[my] country" and now having come back to "wax poetic" about life abroad. Having blurted out her resentments, she then left in the middle of the Q&A. So rare do such public outbursts seem in today's Russia, I could tell the audience viewed her as a specter out of the Soviet past.

Where, then, have the Russian antisemites gone?

Of course, outspoken antisemites are alive and well in Russia's public sphere, most notably in the ranks of

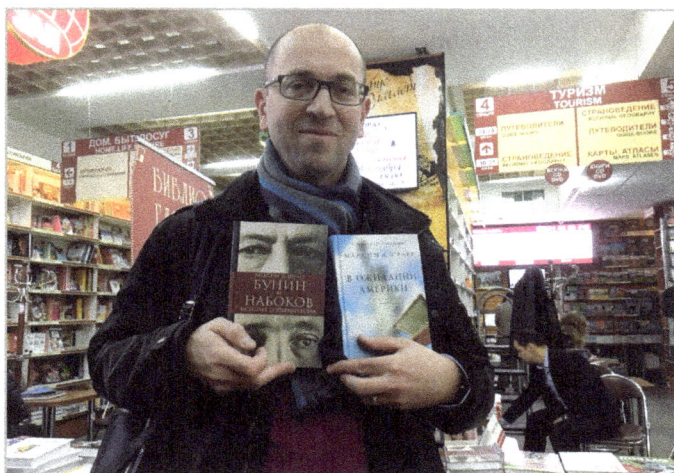

Maxim D. Shrayer holding copies of his books Bunin and Nabokov.
A History of Rivalry *and* Waiting for America *after his reading
at Biblio-Globus Bookstore. Moscow, October 29, 2016.
Photo by Mira Isabella Shrayer.*

Russian nationalists and ultranationalists marching under various church and state banners. In February 2017, Vitaly Milonov, member of the Duma, stated at a public gathering in front of St. Isaac's Cathedral in St. Petersburg: "Christians have survived, even though the ancestors of Boris Lazarovich Vishnevsky and Maksim Lvovich Reznik boiled us in cauldrons and sent [us] to be massacred by wild beasts." In his remarks, Milonov was referring to two local politicians of Jewish origin. Unabashed antisemitism has made something of a comeback in the mainstream of Russian media and politics—consider also the ugly anti-Jewish comments the Duma member Pyotr Tolstoy made in January 2017, accusing the "people who

51

are the grandchildren and great-grandchildren of those who destroyed our churches, who sprung out of the Pale of Settlement with revolvers in 1917," of allegedly continuing to destroy Russian traditions. In these and other statements by Russian civil servants and politicians, commonplaces of prerevolutionary Russian antisemitism are conflated with Soviet-vintage rhetoric against Jews, Judaism, and Israel. Alarmingly, the Kremlin has yet to offer a clear denunciation of such acts of open public prejudice directed against Jews.

For sure, antisemitic poison hasn't been flushed out of Russia's veins. And yet I'm less intrigued by politicians spouting antisemitic rhetoric or by extremists in the open, Russia's professional Jew-haters. Rather, I have in mind the so-called average citizens, the fodder of public opinion surveys. While one is less likely to encounter open and overt expressions of hatred of Jews in the streets, schools, or stadiums, its putrid flowers continue to bloom—openly, pseudonymously or anonymously, and privately—in the space that is about the same age as the new Russia: the Internet and social media. A number of experts at the conference, including Alexander Verkhovsky, director of SOVA Center for Information and Analysis, which monitors xenophobia in Russia, confirmed this. And I've seen it myself: every time I publish something about Russian Jews or give an interview to a Russian media outlet, I receive antisemitic hate mail and Internet posts. (Some of this might be the work of the so-called "Kremlin trolls.")

Who are these people, today's unprejudiced average Russian citizens by day, outspoken antisemites by night? For surely those who choose to channel their dislike of Jews in the liberating environment of an Internet portal aren't a different breed from the Russians who wouldn't think of enacting such sentiments in the traditional public sphere. What is harder to appreciate is not the retreat of Russian antisemitism into the less public and more liberating realm of the Internet and social media, but the Dr. Jekyll and Mr. Hyde effect. The antisemites on the Russian Internet are the same Russians who may not be emboldened to enact open antisemitism in traditional public spheres but practice open prejudice in Russian social networks.

This brings us to the cursed question of implicit bias in surveys of public opinion. A few days after I returned home from Moscow, I was standing by the edge of a soccer field during my younger daughter's weekly practice. I was chatting with a classmate's parent, a Boston-based academic, not Jewish. He listened silently to my account of the recent Russian survey, chewed on the crisp autumn air, and then remarked, "If you were conducting a survey of racism in Boston, it would probably show that it's virtually nonexistent, wouldn't it? Does that mean it's not there?"

4. The Ambassador of Jewish Pride

I met Rabbi Berel Lazar on October 31, 2016, at Spaso House, the palatial residence of U.S. ambassadors to the USSR and Russia since 1934. Ambassador John F. Tefft was hosting a reception for American presenters at the conference on antisemitism. Also invited were political scientists participating in a joint United States–Russia workshop and leaders of Moscow's Jewish community. In his welcoming remarks, the ambassador stressed the relatively low number of antisemitic instances in Russia while—again—cautioning that history teaches us to remain "vigilant."

Sipping bourbon, I approached Rabbi Lazar and introduced myself. We chatted for a few minutes about Boston and about children (he's blessed with thirteen to my two). Then a towering American professor of Jewish studies interrupted to ask if Lazar could recommend a kosher restaurant in Moscow. A smile flickering on his lips, Lazar replied with a question: "What kind are you looking for? Italian? East-European traditional? Israeli? We have many." He then returned to our conversation, in the course of which it emerged that Mira, who was with me at the reception, had the same Hebrew name as one of Rabbi Lazar's own daughters. Two days later I received an email: "It was a pleasure meeting you yesterday at Spaso House. Please send my regards to Miriam Beila."

Rav Berel Lazar and Mira Isabella Shrayer.
Spaso House, Moscow, October 31, 2016.
Photo by Maxim D. Shrayer.

Lazar was born in 1964 in Milan to parents who were in the first cohort of worldwide emissaries sent out by the late Lubavitcher Rebbe. At fifteen he came to the United States to study and be ordained as a rabbi. Arriving in Russia in 1990, the last Soviet year, he soon became rabbi at the Maryina Roshcha synagogue, just a yarmulke's throw from where the Jewish Museum and Tolerance Center would be founded. In 2000 he became a Russian citizen and chief rabbi—a post held jointly by him and the much older, Birobidzhan-born Adolf Shayevich, rabbi of the Moscow Choral Synagogue since 1983 and titular leader of non-Haredi Orthodox Judaism in Russia. Putin's government formally recognizes Berel Lazar as the chief rabbi of Russia and openly favors his organization, the Federation of Jewish Communities of Russia, over Rabbi Shayevich's Congress of Jewish Organizations and Associations. At the Federation of Jewish Communities of Russia, the umbrella organization of some 200 Chabad-led communities, Lazar heads the rabbinical council.

The paradox of the Chabad-Lubavitch movement in Russia lies less in its eschewal of insularity than in its tacit involvement in Russia's mainstream politics and culture. This, I believe, is in part a result of the tireless efforts of the Rebbe's emissaries who began to arrive in the early 1990s with a mandate to revive traditional Jewish education. But there's another side to Chabad's success in Russia. Many of Russian Jewry's core community leaders and rabbis are not the children of foreign-born Hasidim but ex-Soviets who became *baʿalei tʼshuva* (returnees to Judaism) and made a conscious choice not to emigrate. This makes a huge difference in the way they relate to Russia, its people, and its culture.

Back in the 1990s, when I was a graduate student in New Haven, I studied for a while with a tutor from a local Chabad yeshiva. This very smart American-born young man had virtually no idea of American or Western culture and literature. When I asked him, innocently, whether he read Jewish writers—Kafka, Malamud, Babel—he replied, "We have our own great stories." This would not happen in Russia today, where many Chabad activists are Pushkin-quoting men and women in Hasidic attire.

How big is Russia's Chabad-Lubavitch community? Accounts vary, depending on which circles are included and on the person doing the counting. A self-identified *baʿalat tʼshuva* who is married to a Jewish community worker in St. Petersburg, a city with some 27,000 Jews, estimates that 30–50 families form the core of their community. Yakov Ratner, a Moscow-based member of the Chabad community (we'll meet him later), put the number of families at 200, and then clarified with a subtler assessment:

> Two hundred is the most general approximation, without separating by citizenship, language, or degree of religious observance beyond being connected with Chabad and known to keep [some of

the commandments]. If you ask how many families whose native language is Russian follow the principal practices of Chabad, my estimate would be 50. But it's an estimate, not research data.

That's 50 families out of about 61,000 Jews in Moscow. Demographers and sociologists offer similar and sometimes lower estimates. Experts on Jewish education and parents of students enrolled at Russia's religious schools praise the unique quality of such institutions as Yeshiva Ktana Chabad Lubavitch outside Moscow, where about 100 students live and learn.

The historian Galina Zelenina recently published a fascinating analysis of the Jewish spectrum in today's Russia, based on qualitative data gathered from Moscow Jews. Liberal or Reform Judaism is still regarded with skepticism, as something of a foreign sect. Modern Orthodoxy is often viewed through a prism of nostalgia for the days when the Moscow Choral Synagogue and the steep street on which it stands in the center of Moscow betokened both the past and the present of Soviet Jewry. At the same time, many of today's Russian Jews identify Chabad-Lubavitch as a force that rules religious and communal life—a role that is much more central and mainstream than that of its sister organizations in Western Europe or the Americas. Similarly, an average Russian citizen is also much likelier to identify Rabbi Lazar, the Italian-born Hasid, as the symbol of today's Russian

Jews. An average US citizen would probably think of Larry David.

Berel Lazar is an elegant dresser, with a dash of Milanese fashion. A perfectly cut *kapoteh* (frock coat) hugs his slender frame. Small elongated glasses, their lower part rimless, accentuate his pale, aristocratic brow. On the evening I met him, he was sporting a black and silver tie with a mesh pattern. He walks like a soccer player, with a springy gait. His long, pointed, graying beard drawing attention to his youthful, unwrinkled face. When you speak with him, you notice the twinkle first, then become aware of other worlds orbiting in his eyes. Wit and charm come naturally to Lazar, both in Russian and in English, the two languages I heard him speak. Asked by a TV journalist about the budget of the Russian Jewish Congress, he replied without so much as a flinch, "Much less than what you think and much more than what I think."

In a column published in *Lekhaim*, Lazar reflected on the August 2016 convention of European Chabad-Lubavitch rabbis, held in Russia. About 100 rabbis were in attendance, and they wanted to visit Liozna and Liady, sites holy to the movement but located on the other side of the Russian border in Belarus. "We arrive in Lubavitch," writes Lazar, using the Yiddish name for the town where Chabad's early leaders lived, and "pray at the grave of Rebbe Tzemach Tzedek and

Rebbe Maharash." But no provision had been made for crossing into Belarus:

> We understand that we don't have a choice, we must drive to the border, and then—however G-d disposes. We arrive, we wait for the decision: wait an hour, wait another hour. . . . And then—completely by chance!—I get a call from our great friend. . . . And in a little while the long-awaited permission arrives: "As an exception, the column of buses is to be allowed through.". . . Many rabbis later admitted they didn't think the outcome would be successful: what happened at the last minute, they were saying, was a true miracle!

For Rabbi Lazar, it seems, Jews in Russia are not G-d's mistake. However G-d may test His people, He doesn't make mistakes. G-d disposes, and Russia's political leaders make the necessary arrangements, including exceptions to Russian visa regulations.

The following evening (November 1, 2016), I had another chance to observe Lazar in action when he gave a seven-minute address at the banquet for the participants and guests of the conference on antisemitism. Levitating to the podium, he asked, in fluent Russian, whether to speak in Russian or English. After an opening joke he switched to English and began with a recollection (I quote from a recording of Lazar's speech):

4. The Ambassador of Jewish Pride

I remember around 30 years ago when I first came to Moscow, the Soviet Union was then still going strong. . . . And I asked an old Jewish lady, "Tell me, are there any Jewish books here?" The people were even afraid to talk then. No answer. I asked her, "Is there kosher food?" Still no answer. "Are there Jewish schools?" No answer. . . . "Tell me, is there antisemitism in Russia?" She says, "Rebbe, here there is nothing. *U nas nichego net.*"

Nothing, *nichego, gornisht*: the word was meant to sum up 70 Soviet years that, in this reckoning, saw a near-total destruction of traditional Jewish life and Jewish learning. Lazar's anecdote fashioned the mission of Chabad-Lubavitch not as a renewal but almost as a reinvention of public Jewish life. Not only the official remnants of Judaism (embodied in the Moscow Choral Synagogue and its "Soviet" rabbis) but even the underground or barely above ground work of the Chabadnik activists who remained in the USSR vanished in the narrative. The unsanctioned grassroots movement of Jewish learning in the 1960s–80s, made possible by refusenik zealots, didn't receive mention, either. In Lazar's narrative arc, only with the arrival of the Rebbe's emissaries in the early 1990s was Jewish life rebuilt almost from ground zero until the point where, today, Chabad-Lubavitch stands as the guardian of Russia's Jews.

Rabbi Lazar's seamlessly delivered speech focused on three points. First, he offered a brief summary of what has been accomplished over the past 30 years:

> The question that everybody asks is: "How did it happen? Tell us the secret. How could you change the tide of what's going on today in Europe?" One point that very often is left out is a strong Jewish community. A proud Jewish community. An active Jewish community. People respect us when we show that we are not hiding our identity, when we are teaching our children the values of our tradition, when we show that we're united and we care, and . . . we're not going to stay silent.

Second, Lazar linked the success and safety of Russia's Jewish community with the benefaction of the Russian government:

> Different leaders around the world have to understand that it's their responsibility to watch over any minority, especially the Jewish people who have suffered so much in the last century. . . . And I'm sure that today during the conference this issue was brought up, and I'm sure that Mr. Putin got the credit he deserves for standing strong and doing whatever can be done to show that Russia will not tolerate any antisemitism.

Lazar's final point concerned the public profile of Jews in today's Russia:

> One of the most important things is education. Not only educating our own children but educating the people around us. I think the Jewish community in Russia has done a lot to open its doors, to tell people what we stand for, what are our values, what we believe in, and how we care about the country we live in. The moment people see that we are equal citizens in our responsibilities and in our actions, I think they will respect us even more.

Following Rabbi Lazar's speech, a Dostoevskian scene occurred, straight out of *The Possessed*. Aleksandr Minkin, a columnist at the Russian daily *Moskovsky Komsomolets*, made his way to the podium. The seventy-year-old Minkin, who looks a bit like what I imagine Judah Maccabee looked like and a bit like a tired actor in a provincial Russian theater, is nationally recognized for his diatribes against corruption in Russia and for his past closeness to the exiled oligarch Vladimir Gusinsky, a principal player in the Russian Jewish Congress until he fell out with Putin.

Minkin's remarks appeared to be unscripted, but they deflated the evening's rhetorical balloons. Here's a literal English translation: "Those of you who [visit] Facebook or some social media . . . see the totally beastly bared teeth of

Nazism and, in particular, of antisemitism. . . . It is completely impossible to speak with such mellowness of how . . . everything here [in Russia] has become wonderful, how there is nothing dangerous here."

Minkin then recalled a visit to Russia by the late Shimon Peres, who spoke with pride about the 1991 Operation Solomon in which 35 planes airlifted over 14,000 Ethiopian Jews to Israel in 36 hours. Minkin said he asked the Israeli president, "Do you know how many Jews there are in Russia? . . . And how many airplanes and how many trains it would take to rescue them?" In Russia, he now admonished those present, people were "living on top of a volcano" that could erupt at any time. "And if it happens," Minkin predicted, "nobody will be able to help the Jews of Russia, even if they wanted to."

5. Staying or Leaving

For me as an ex-Soviet Jew, a map of Moscow is not only a map of childhood and first love but also a map of antisemitism. And a return to my native city is a visit to a place that now seems both much more tolerant and more foreign, because it's in the Soviet past that I still strangely belong. When I show my daughters around Moscow, I'm conflicted about which of the two maps to unfold, which memories to suppress.

On a Saturday morning, as Mira and I entered the metro and rode the long escalator down to the platform, I found myself in the grip of an anguished recollection. I was twelve, the age when budding adolescence would bring out the Levantine features on the faces of Jewish boys and girls. To a phenotypically trained Soviet eye—and most Soviet citizens were keen ethnographers—I *looked* Jewish. And like Isaac Babel's preteen protagonist who transgressed Jewish customs and dreamed of breeding doves, I, too, dreamed of breeding wildlife—not birds but veiltail betta fish. Parti-colored, feisty, they came from tropical Siam and beckoned a young breeder away from wintry Moscow to realms wondrous and unknown.

I belonged to a group of kids who gathered once a week at the Moscow Palace of Young Pioneers, where a female graduate student in biology directed our ichthyological explorations. One cold Sunday, it must have been in 1979, five of us went to Ptichiy Rynok (literally: Bird Market), an outdoor area where various pets were sold by breeders. I was the only Jew in the group. Three boys had Russian or Ukrainian last names, one a Korean name. The boy's Korean ancestors had been exiled from the Far East to Central Asia; his father eventually made it to Moscow and married an ethnic Russian woman.

After shopping for aqueous treasures, each of us ended up with a small glass jar containing one or two tropical fish. It was winter, and we had to carry the jars close to our bodies, in breast pockets or close to armpits, wrapped in scarves or gloves. Elated with our purchases, we ran to the nearest metro stop and got on the escalator.

At this point, just as in a dark fairy tale—except it was absolutely true—a Russian lady materialized next to our group. She was what one might call a Soviet Russian everywoman: about sixty-five, a gray woolen headscarf, a swampy coat of coarse wool, earrings with synthetic corundum, mesh sack with groceries in her left hand. She came straight at me, grabbed me by the hood of my jacket, and started yelling with rabid conviction, "Look at you kikes, you don't go to school, you don't work. Well, soon they'll kick you out of here, send you places." She was pulling hard at my hood as the escalator descended, and I was trying to protect the glass jar with my veiltail betta fish as the other boys stood by and watched. Finally I overcame my stupor, jerked and ripped the hood from her clutches, and yelled back, "Shut up!" That was all I could muster. As we waited for the train on the platform, the part-Korean boy patted me on the shoulder and said, "It's going to be okay." The others just stood there, eyes glued to the veiny marble of the station floor.

I've written a whole book, *Leaving Russia: A Jewish Story*, about growing up Jewish in the former USSR, and I thought I'd put it all behind me. But trips to Moscow, and especially this past visit with Mira—a visit framed by thoughts and discussions about antisemitism—proved that I can't let go. Nor can I stop asking myself the same two-winged question: Why do Jews stay in Russia? Why are they defying history? The question forms something of a chasm between ex-Soviet Jews, especially former refuseniks such as my family, and those who have elected to remain. Among the latter, the only exceptions are three or four close friends in Moscow and St. Petersburg whose lives and circumstances I understand almost as well as my own.

So why are they staying, or are they in fact just waiting to leave? It's of course easy to understand the situation of a successful Jewish venture capitalist who is developing state-of-the-art IT company in Siberia. It's also not hard to understand the reluctance of elderly Russian Jews to uproot themselves now. And I'm fully aware of the reasons why members of Russia's Chabad-Lubavitch community are committed to Jewish life in Russia, even though they might send their sons to continue their studies at a yeshiva in the UK, Israel, or America. But what about others in their twenties, thirties, forties, and fifties? Why do they stay?

In the course of my most recent visit, I initiated a number of conversations on this point. I told my contacts I wanted to quote their responses in an American magazine, and not all of them wished to be quoted in print. (One of the original interviewees later asked me to withdraw her comments, originally published in *Mosaic Magazine*, from the book.) Of course, personal circumstances or contingencies sometimes determine the outcome of qualitative interviews. At the same time, many Jews in today's Russia felt that things could quickly get much worse for the Jewish community if the current regime were overhauled and the current Kremlin leaders replaced with even more Russocentric politicians. I also learned that there were Jews who were reluctant to go on record discussing not only antisemitism in today's Russia but also the legacy of the refusenik movement and of the Jewish exodus from the Soviet Union. Such a reluctance strikes me as concordant with the public amnesia in today's Russia of the systematic persecution of Jews in the late Soviet period. It may also reflect a limited educational exposure of the Russian population to the dark and sorrowful pages in the history of Jews in Russia and the former Soviet Union.

As a result, some of the conversations about the present and future of Russia's Jews went nowhere and had to be abandoned. Others, however, became very productive and continued in written form after my return home to Boston. For reasons of generational dynamics, I resolved to focus on Jews roughly between the ages of thirty-six and fifty-six—that is, born no earlier than 1960 and no later than 1980. Even though I aimed for diversity, there was an inevitable randomness and self-selection in my interviewees, who in part reflected the circles of my acquaintances.

I ended up with seven interviewees: four men and three women. I asked a single set of questions: "Why do Jews continue to live in Russia, after everything they'd been through? What are the prospects of Jewish life in Russia? What lies ahead? What awaits the children born to Jews of this generation who haven't left?"

Below are translated selections from the answers, arranged in descending order of age.

Afanasy Mamedov (born 1960)—lives in Moscow; fiction and nonfiction writer, magazine editor; interviewed on November 16, 2016:

> Oy, . . . I feel like speaking with the intonation of [the satirist Mikhail] Zhvanetsky: "It's quiet for the time being, but only for the time being." . . . And when they come up to you and ask how to get to such and such an address and you know

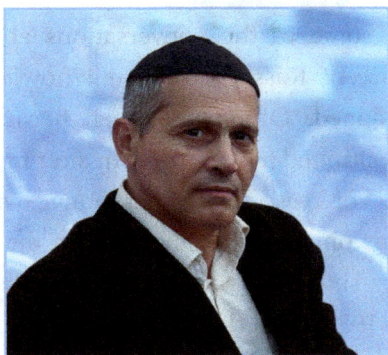

Photo by Vadim Brodsky

they mean a synagogue or the Jewish Museum and Tolerance Center, for some reason you immediately start inquiring about the weather in Tel Aviv and the airfare.

The future of Jewish life and Jewish culture in Russia depends on a number of factors but chiefly on the state of the "Jewish question" and on whether the Jewish community will have funds. Many confuse [Jewish culture] with the religious tradition, the communal life, which is, in my view, fundamentally incorrect. . . . Where are our own Jewish writers? . . . What is being done to foster their existence? In order for us to have our own Malamuds, Roths, and Bellows, . . . we should in all sorts of ways nurture the writers we already have. . . . There are different ways of solving this problem. For instance, to institute a prize. But I haven't heard of any Jewish literary prizes [in Russia]. There isn't a single café for Jewish intelligentsia to congregate. . . . Hebrew classes at the synagogue or fitness facilities could hardly address this problem. . . .

One could say, "What is 20 years of freedom? Wait, it's all on the way." But one wants it now and more of it. I think Jewish cultural life in Russia depends on direct philanthropy. We don't have our own [Jewish] Morozovs and Tretyakovs [major Russian philanthropists and patrons of the arts in the second half of the nineteenth century]. . . . I doubt the situation is going to change any time soon, and the birth of the next Kafka is unlikely here. . . . Everything is still rising from the old yeast.

Boris Lanin (born 1961)—lives in Moscow; professor and literary scholar, Russia's leading expert on Vasily Grossman, author of a series of middle-school and high-school textbooks; interviewed on November 15, 2016:

There are probably several categories of [Jews] and therefore several [sets of] answers. Group (1) are afraid of leaving; group (2) are comfortable in Russia; group (3) have identity problems and don't consider themselves Jewish; group (4) are at anchor, held here by somebody or something; and group (5) will leave eventually, one day.

Photo Irina Radzinskaya

Two days later, on November 17, 2016, Lanin sent a follow-up comment:

> Really, what am I doing here? . . . Well at least here I'm a full professor, and I haven't found another place for myself in the world. . . . My parents immigrated to Israel from Baku. They lived in poverty. I visited Israel for the first time in October 1991, eleven months after their departure. . . . My father, a violinist, was driving a garbage truck; my mother helped the elderly do their shopping. Both of my parents were then fifty-four. I found nothing for myself [in Israel], and later there were also no prospects for me there.
>
> It would seem as if it's high time to go, but at the same time here I'm the author of eight textbooks, with annual sales of 100,000 copies in the last two years. And who will I be in Israel? A retiree,

a complete nobody. I'm almost fifty-five, and I still haven't left. . . .

Yet now I feel that my textbooks will be banned—and then emigration will once again be on the agenda.

Photo by Vasily Rusanov

Anna Narinskaya (born 1966)—lives in Moscow; book critic, essayist, former columnist at *Kommersant-Daily*. When Narinskaya was seven years old, she was baptized together with her parents in the Russian Orthodox Church. She also baptized both of her own children but told me that she hadn't been to church in fifteen years because of her "differences, not so much with the Russian Orthodox Church as with church as an institution in general"; interviewed on November 29, 2016:

It's not entirely clear what it means to be a "Jew" in Russia. In Soviet times passports had the [mandated] nationality line, so people far removed from Judaism or the Jewish tradition were considered (or considered themselves) Jews. Many in the 1970s and 1980s even converted to Orthodox Christianity, as back then it was a form of [protest]. [In 2007, in *An Anthology of Jewish-Russian Literature*, I estimated that "several thousand" Soviet Jews converted to Christianity in the 1960s-1980s.— M.D.S.] Which is why today's "Jews" in Russia are people of 100-percent Russian culture. Where can they go?

Jewish culture in its religious-traditional sense will always be on a "reservation" here [in Russia]. The fate of "Jewish" children (that is, Jewish by blood) isn't different from the fate of children of other members of the intelligentsia. They will be leaving. But most likely not for Israel but for Europe or America.

Dmitry Bavilsky (born 1969)—lives in Moscow; novelist, journalist, art critic. Dmitry's father is a professor of medicine. His parents live in Chelyabinsk, an industrial city in the southern Urals. His sister and her family live in Ramat Gan, Israel; interviewed on November 14, 2016:

Fromtimetotime I think about [emigrating], but I'm still holding out. There are some basic indicators that I keep in mind. There are definite boundaries,

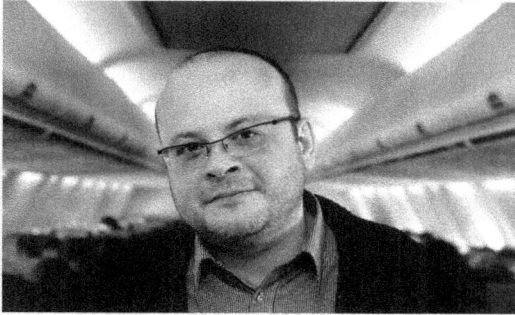

Photo by Sergei Golovach

important for me, which the state hasn't yet crossed (Internet, freedom to come and go, a certain income level). My professional responsibilities have to do with the Russian language, which is why emigration for me is an extremely complicated and painful issue, which I would like to be able to avoid.

The current of the Jewish question in postmodern Russia runs feebly and slowly. There's the inexorable, archetypal legacy of the past, from which there's no escape, but for the time being it's bottled up or dispersed, and it seems that the designation of "Other" in today's Russia has been given to people from the Caucasus and gays. That is to say, in the conditions of a dispersed and atrophied society, and without any targeted efforts from above, the Jewish question is, perhaps, temporarily closed.

Fewer and fewer Jews remain in Russia. I think that their (our) number will continue to decrease.

Without any specially targeted adverse ideological actions (sanctioned persecution), the [Jewish] question will not be deliberately enunciated [as a question]. In this sense, Russian Jews share the common fate of all of postimperial Russia.

Photo by Zalman Ratner

Yakov Ratner (born 1973)—lives in Moscow; Chabad community member; director of the publishing house Knizhniki (Moscow) and administrative director of *Lekhaim* magazine; interviewed on November 14, 2016, and June 2–5, 2017:

In my view not all people plan their lives in terms of strategic historical paradigms. Many base their perceptions on the present moment while relying in much else on . . . favorable circumstances. This way, the deciding factors could stem not from an objective (however objective it may be) multifactorial analysis but from personal possibilities, habits, predilections, interests, milieu, down to obligations and present-day tasks. And this isn't necessarily bad, depending on the goals of the specific individuals. I don't know. . . . I think that this is unpredictable, as is our economy and domestic politics. Some of the people, just as is the case elsewhere in the world, will deepen their identity, while others will dilute it. I hope [Russia] will be an ordinary country within the main currents of Europe.

I'm not entirely sure what "Jews of Russia" means. Orthodox communities? What awaits them, perhaps, is cultural survival. In terms of Russian reality the term "Orthodox communities" describes a social circle and also includes secular Jews involved in the activities of the Orthodox community, through religions programs and through education, leisure, and so forth. . . . The perspectives for secular Jews are comparable with the perspectives for [Russia's] entire educated population: a liberal ideological platform, cosmopolitanism in terms of work and residence, susceptibility to the influence of economic declines. My acquaintances among [secular Jews] in their vast majority have dual [Russian and Israeli] citizenship but remain connected to Russia. They do not share the official ideology but tend not to get involved in political activities; they seek to structure their existence as their interests and circumstances dictate. The important part is that their ties with Jewishness depend indirectly, yet tangibly, on the development of the national (Orthodox) community, with which they align their identity as Jews. . . .

[The future of Jewish children] depends on their parents. All opportunities from secular schools to cheders now exist in large [Russian] cities. The Israeli intolerance of ultra-Orthodox Jews [Ratner used the derogatory Israeli Hebrew slang term *dos*, plural *dosim,* to illustrate his point] does not weigh heavily on the children here, which is very important. Now in Diaspora, a child simultaneously sees a complete legitimacy of Jewishness (museums, theaters, individual people), a normal existence of the Orthodox tradition with its voluntary distinctiveness, and, finally, a broad and varied use of [Jewish] traditions in daily living practice. But if the parents are not interested in identity as such (which very often and commonly comes from a dearth of [Jewish] education over many generations), then only chance could carry such a child [toward Jewishnes]—chance coupled with something very deeply seated, something that would then be activated.

Photo by Pavel Charny

Anna Bokshitskaya (born 1978)—lives in Moscow; a journalist by training with extensive background in publishing; presently executive director of the Russian Jewish Congress; interviewed on November 20, 2016:

> Even in times of extreme need, . . . many people decide to stay and wait it out. I remember, in my childhood, when antisemitism was in full bloom, emigration paperwork would regularly turn up in our home—to America, Denmark, Germany, and even Australia, any place where they might have suddenly started accepting Jews. We filled out the paperwork but we didn't leave . . . because of the family, elderly parents (who were still alive!). What's now been added to the mix is that in this country the situation with antisemitism has radically changed. Moreover, strange as it

sounds, it's become fashionable to be a Jew. People look for their Jewish roots. It would seem that to some extent we have now attained the results that many Jewish organizations have been working to achieve.

Accordingly. . . . people are more unwilling to leave the place where they were born and everything is dear and familiar. . . . Now a Jewish life exists in Russia in all its forms and expressions—what the Russian Jewish Congress strives for and supports—and further growth and development are indicated. . . .

There's one more factor. Many Jews living in Russia have long since obtained Israeli citizenship, and those who haven't done so already are living with the sense that if something were to happen, they would manage to obtain it. That is: it's as though we don't have to go, all's well, but should something happen, we'll be able to go.

Jewish children . . . have grown up with the understanding that the world is open and one can go and study, go and live, anywhere. My feeling is that their heads are set up differently and they don't ponder this question. . . . But still it's important to add that, even though at the present time antisemitism in Russia is low and the situation is calm, we continue to monitor the situation constantly . . . because Jews, unfortunately (or fortunately), have too good a memory simply to close their eyes and not look around them.

Photo by Nir Turgeman

Finally, while working on this book I saw a Facebook post by one of my contacts, **Dasha Kholobaeva** (born 1984), a journalist who had previously lived in Moscow and served as managing editor of the opposition website *Open Russia*. Her post, dated November 20, 2016, read:

> Dear Friends, I've moved to Israel . . . and settled in Haifa. Forgive me, those to whom I didn't have a chance to say goodbye. . . . I miss you and hope to see you in different cities and countries. It's warm here, the sea right nearby is humming, and the lighthouse is blinking. . . . One of the strongest impressions: armed people who aren't at all scary. And one thinks all sorts of new thoughts about

the homeland. I hug you and love you, until I see you again.

Dasha Kholobaeva has one Jewish grandparent. She grew up in Moscow, studied in Berlin and Prague. At the time of writing she was studying Hebrew at an *ulpan* in Israel. I was so intrigued by her post that I invited her to answer the same questions I'd posed to my six respondents. Here's what she wrote back on November 21, 2016:

> I've never personally experienced antisemitism.... But in Russia I was surrounded by a very decent social circle, which had been in the making for a number of years, and I simply cannot imagine aggressive antisemitism coming from one of my acquaintances. On the other hand, in recent years the temperature of xenophobia in Russia is notably rising, people are becoming nastier, and yes, one can encounter antisemitism along with other unwelcoming expressions pouring from propaganda loudspeakers or simply in the streets.
>
> Why do they stay? Why do we all live? I'm not sure there's a higher meaning. [Many] don't leave because they have grown used to Russia, I think, although I've also heard that of late a great many have been leaving for Israel (and not only Israel). It's like asking why descendants of victims

of [Stalinist] repressions are living in Russia. Probably because they were born there, and they don't have a great desire to move to another country, or if they have the desire, then a fear of change outweighs it. . . .

[For me personally] there were several reasons and motivations. I'm an editor and journalist, and journalism in Russia has nearly disappeared. The best publications (and I've worked for several) have in recent years either been shut down or been changed by censorship beyond recognition. . . . Perhaps above all else was the feeling of too little freedom and too much suffering all around. After Crimea and the war with Ukraine, this feeling has become more acute. . . .

6. Almost Folklore

When I was a refusenik teenager in Moscow, I heard maudlin jokes about Jewish emigration. One of them told of a special voice recording created at the Visa Office. You dialed the main number and heard "*zhdite otkaza*" (wait for your request to be denied) instead of the conventional "*zhdite otveta*" (wait for your call to be answered). This hangman's joke reflected the hopeless atmosphere of the early 1980s, when emigration was at a near standstill and about 1.7 million Jews remained in the USSR. Another refusenik joke betokened a Jew's undying hope of getting out of Russia by designating the last, legendary Jewish woman in the entire city of Leningrad. Her name was Aurora Kruiser, and she, too, was getting ready to weigh anchor. (If you don't get the joke—and Soviet jokes, even Soviet *Jewish* jokes, are an acquired habit and don't work well in translation—let me explain. *Aurora* is the name of a Russian cruiser that in 1905 survived the Battle of Tsushima, was eventually returned to the Baltic Fleet, and in October 1917 allegedly fired a blank shot to start the assault on the Winter Palace. After World War II, *Aurora* was permanently anchored on the Neva and became a museum.) I also recall a futuristic joke depicting a street scene in 2020. A boy and his father are walking in the center of Moscow. The boy pulls his father by the sleeve and points to an older lady rushing along: "Look, dad, I think it's a Jew." The lady stops, looks the boy in the eye, and wails, "I'm not a Jew, I'm a madwoman."

Jokes of this sort have become a vestige of the Soviet past along with the mandatory "fifth" (nationality) line in the passport and with manifestations of "streetcar" antisemitism. Not only Jewish jokes of the Soviet era are disappearing. Jewish faces and Jewish names are starting to vanish from the Russian mainstream—from literature, the arts, and the entertainment industry but also from the achievement rolls of sciences, medicine, and the humanities. This seems especially true for Russia's millennials.

Despite all the advances of the post-Soviet years, despite what appears to be state patronage of sorts and even the reputation of a protected minority, despite the low incidence of public antisemitism, and despite the strength of communal, religious, and educational institutions, Russia's Jewish community is indeed shrinking. Today's core Jewish population of under 180,000 puts Russia behind Israel and the U.S. by millions and also behind France, Canada, and the UK. True, the numbers still more or less equal those of the Jewish community of Argentina and edge out those in Germany, Australia, and Brazil. But will Russian Jews remain in the top ten, or will they eventually slide to the level of Belgium, Italy, Switzerland, and Chile, all in the range of 20,000–30,000?

With about 7,000 new arrivals in 2016, emigration from Russia to Israel (the only country that accepts Jews by default) increased by about 5 percent over the previous year. (Mark Tolts estimates a steeper increase of 11 percent for the first first half of 2017.) Russia'a remaining Jewish population is declining and aging. Outside the relatively small community of the ultra-Orthodox, the median age of Russian Jews is about sixty and the birthrate is the lowest of any ethnic group, significantly below replacement level. (For purposes of comparison, the median Jewish age in the United States is about forty and the level of childbirth is 1.9 children per Jewish woman; and in Israel, about thirty-two and the level of childbirth is 2.9 per Jewish woman, with the Jewish birthrate well above replacement level.)

Such trends mean that—as a number of my respondents suggest and in a kind of finale to the great story told by the Jewish Museum and Tolerance Center—Jewish names are also starting to disappear from the mainstream of Russian culture and the arts and from the achievement rosters in science and the humanities. Jews are less and less known to—and knowable by—the average Russian. The effect of this on public attitudes is as yet uncertain, but according to the Levada Center study, "the majority of Russian citizens (61 percent today, up from 52 percent in 1990) do not personally know any Jews (among family, relatives, close acquaintances, or colleagues), which is why opinions about them are mostly figments of 'social imagination,' almost folklore."

Almost folklore: in Russia today, there's an official story, which is heartening and positive, adhered to by the regime and by many Jewish community leaders and activists. And then there's what might be thought of as a coded story, whispered by some, or perhaps many, of the Jews still remaining in the community's diminishing population base and whispered back into their ears by memory and by history.

If there's another lesson here, it's one of resisting closure. The great outflux of Jews from the former USSR and the post-Soviet states has changed—perhaps transformed—the living space of world Jewry. With over one million Russian-speaking Jews in Israel, about 500,000 in the United States and Canada, and over 100,000 in Germany, the critical mass of Russian-speaking Jews resides outside Russia's borders. A recent volume, edited by Zvi Gitelman, regards the Russian-speaking immigrants in North America, Israel, and Germany as the "new Jewish Diaspora." While the great history of Russia's Jewish community may be approaching its finale, the legacy of Russia's Jews is vibrantly alive and remains an active story in Israel and America.

In Closing: Jewish Clowns in Moscow

Is it time to compose an elegy for Russia's Jewry?

I pondered this question during the visit to Moscow detailed in these pages. On October 30, 2016, Mira and I watched a circus performance at the Nikulin Circus on Tsvetnoy ("Flower") Boulevard—Moscow's "old" circus. A flood of childhood circus memories carried me back to a different era, the Soviet late 1970s. When I was eleven, my older daughter's present age, I went through a phase of wanting to be a circus performer. Through the poet Ilya Selvinsky, my father knew his stepdaughter Tsetsiliya Voskresenskaya, who was on the faculty of the Moscow College of Circus Arts. One time she invited us to a performance and took me backstage to meet the gymnasts and clowns in training.

At the circus Mira and I were guests of my close friend Maxim Mussel, grandson of three Jews and an ethnic Russian. In 1990 my friend was about to make *aliyah* but changed his mind at the last minute. He started a successful marketing business, married a Russian woman, had two kids, and Mira was now sitting next to Maxim's teenage daughter, a lovely Russian girl who looks more and more

Bella and Alex Cher. Nikulin Circus, Moscow, October 30, 2016.
Photo by Maxim D. Shrayer.

like the Jews in her family. As the band played the opening number, I perused the program, searching for and not finding Jewish names among the circus performers. And then I saw this: "With you the whole evening is the Comic Duo 'Club House'—Bella and Alex Cher." The long program was in Russian, yet the names of the clowns were printed in English. The clowns were a man and a woman in their early forties, both clad in black, white, and red, and both sported matching, large round spectacles with heavy frames. The she-clown wore an apron with many pockets, and she appeared on stage carrying a broom, like a custodial lady intent on cleaning up her partner's slapstick mess. The jokes had a distinctly melancholy tone, as if pointing to a different political climate, when laughing always meant both something less and something more than what it

Maxim Mussel.
Nikulin Circus, Moscow,
October 30, 2016.
Photo by Maxim D. Shrayer.

means in present-day Russia. The whole clowning routine was charming and occasionally quite funny but also pierced with longing for the glory of Soviet circus arts. I was intrigued by the names of the performers, which made me think of Sonny and Cher. Yet to an average Russian in the audience, the English spelling and the sound of the names signaled foreignness and un-Russianness. Probably Jewishness, too. A closer examination of the other side of the program revealed that the last name of the duo of clowns is "Chervotkin," and that in Russia "Alex" used to be Aleksandr, and "Bella" used to be Elena. I later discovered that Aleksandr Chervotkin (aka "Alex Cher") actually came from a prominent Russian family of actors and circus entertainers. In the late 1990s, the couple had moved to the United States to tour with American circuses and adopted a new stage name. Some fifteen years later, they were invited to perform in Russia, now appearing there as Bella and Alex Cher.

In the old Soviet days, quite a few Jews adopted Russian pennames and stage names to bypass antisemitism and not to "stick out." But Jewish names are in vogue in today's Russia, and expatriate clowns with a Jewish-sounding stage name now amuse Russian audiences. Do the real Elena and Aleksandr Chervotkin have Jewish ancestors? They apparently do not, but that isn't really the point. In Russia, a country continuously losing its real Jews, Bella and Alex Cher are playing the part of imaginary Jewish clowns. Is Russia, then, laughing at her Jews? With her Jews? Laughing without Jews?

I wanted to interview the duo of clowns who amused the Russian audience with bitter-sweet Jewish humor. I sent them several emails and Facebook messages with questions. Eight months have gone by, and I'm still waiting for an answer.

December 2016-July 2017
Brookline–South Chatham, Mass.

Acknowledgments

The materials for this book were initially collected on October 28–November 3, 2016, during a visit to Moscow. I would like to thank the organizers of the Moscow International Conference on Combating Antisemitism (2016) for inviting me to present a paper and moderate a panel. My special thanks go to Genesis Philanthropy Group and its president and CEO, Ilia Salita, for their support.

Boston College provided partial funding for this trip and assisted with the publication of this book, and I wish to express my appreciation to Gregory Kalscheur, S.J., dean of the Morrissey College of Arts and Sciences, and to Tom Chiles, vice provost for research.

Neal Kozodoy, editor of *Mosaic Magazine*, where an earlier version of much of this book was originally published as an essay of the month, provided brilliant editorial comments. Jonathan Zalman, editor of *The Scroll* rubric of *Tablet Magazine*, published an early version of the concluding section of the book and offered valuable suggestions. Would that all editors were so generous with their insights.

I am grateful to Dobrochna (Dosia) Fire for a stellar copyediting job, to Ivan Grave for designing a beautiful cover, and to the staff of Academic Studies Press—Matthew Charlton, Oleh Kotsyuba, Kira Nemirovsky, Igor Nemirovsky and others—for welcoming the book and giving it a home in Beantown.

A number of friends and colleagues contributed to the making of this project, and I gratefully acknowledge their assistance: Liya Chechik; Oleg Dorman; Gennady Estraykh; Boruch Gorin; Olga Kononova; Maxim Mussel; Alisa Nagrodskaya; Yekaterina Tsarapkina. Several individuals, whose opinions informed my research and writing, have requested not to be identified in the text.

Mark Tolts, the leading demographer of Jews in post-Soviet space, generously responded to my queries and shared his expertise.

I was fortunate to have the cooperation of seven remarkable individuals who agreed to be interviewed for this project: Dmitry Bavilsky, Anna Bokshitskaya, Dasha Kholobaeva, Boris Lanin, Afanasy Mamedov, Anna Narinskaya, Yakov Ratner.

Without the support, love, and wisdom of my wife, Karen E. Lasser, daughters Mira Isabella and Tatiana Rebecca, and parents, Emilia Shrayer and David Shrayer-Petrov, my life would be empty and lonely. Their voices and silences are in many pages of this book.

List of Photos

Works Cited

Budnitsky, Oleg. "Oleg Budnitskii Responds to Olga Gershenson's 'The Jewish Museum and Tolerance Center in Moscow: Judaism for the Masses.'" *East European Jewish Affairs* 46, no. 2 (2016): 211–13.

Gershenson, Olga. "The Jewish Museum and Tolerance Center in Moscow: Judaism for the Masses." *East European Jewish Affairs* 45, no. 2–3 (2015): 158–73.

———. "Olga Gershenson's Response." *East European Jewish Affairs* 46, no. 2 (2016): 216–17.

Gitelman, Zvi, ed. *The New Jewish Diaspora: Russian-Speaking Immigrants in the United States, Israel, and Germany*. New Brunswick, NJ: Rutgers University Press, 2016.

Gorin, Boruch. "The Jewish Museum and Tolerance Center." *East European Jewish Affairs* 46, no. 2 (2016): 217–20.

"Jewish Agency, Aliyah and Immigration Ministry Release Aliyah Data for 2016." The Jewish Agency for Israel. December 29, 2016. http://www.jewishagency.org/news/27000-new-israelis. Viewed May 29, 2017.

Klier John Doyle. "Outline of Jewish-Russian History." Part I in Shrayer, ed. *An Anthology of Jewish-Russian Literature* Vol. 1: 1182-1191. Part II in Shrayer, ed. *An Anthology of Jewish-Russian Literature*, Vol. 2: 1192-1198.

Lazar, Berl. "Pochemu eto chudo proizoshlo." *Lekhaim* 10 (2016):
7–8.

Shrayer, Maxim D., ed. *An Anthology of Jewish-Russian Literature:
Two Centuries of Dual Identity in Prose and Poetry.* 2 Vols.
1801-2001. Armonk, NY: M.E. Sharpe, 2007.

Shrayer, Maxim D. *Leaving Russia: A Jewish Story.* Syracuse:
Syracuse University Press, 2013.

Shrayer, Maxim D. "The Prospect for Russia's Jews" [essay of the
month]. *Mosaic Magazine*, March 6, 2017. Invited responses
by Konstanty Gebert (March 13, 2017), Leon Aron (March
20, 2017), and Dovid Margolin (March 23, 2017). A response by Maxim D. Shrayer. "Three and a Half Lessons
of Jewish-Russian History." *Mosaic Magazine*, March 27,
2017.

———. "Is It Time to Compose an Elegy for Russia's Jewry?" *Tablet
Magazine*, March 7, 2017. German translation, "Auf der
Suche nach Freiheit: Ist es an der Zeit, einen Nachruf auf
Russlands Juden zu schreiben?" *Die Jüdische Allgemeine*,
March 16, 2017.

Shrayer-Petrov, David. "My Slavic Soul." Tr. from Russian by Maxim
D. Shrayer. In Shrayer, ed. *An Anthology of Jewish-Russian
Literature*, Vol. 2: 1058-59.

Study Report "Anti-Semitism in Today's Russia." Moscow: Levada
Center, 2016.

Tolts, Mark. "Demography of the Contemporary Russian-Speaking
Jewish Diaspora." In Gitelman, ed., 23–40.

———. "Evrei na postsovetskom prostranstve: novye demogra-
ficheskie dannye." *Demoskop Weekly* 693–94 (August 22–
September 4, 2016): 1–22.

Zelenina, Galina. "Portret na stene i shproty na khlebe: moskovskie
evrei mezhdu dvumia 'sektami.'" *Gosudarstvo, religiia,
tserkov' v Rossii i za rubezhom* 33. no. 4 (2015): 121–69.

Index of Names

Photo by Lee Pellegrini

About the Author

The bilingual author and scholar Maxim D. Shrayer was born in Moscow in 1967 to a Jewish-Russian family and spent almost nine years as a refusenik. He and his parents, the writer and doctor David Shrayer-Petrov and the translator Emilia Shrayer, left the USSR and immigrated to the United States in 1987 after spending a summer in Austria and Italy. Shrayer attended Moscow University, Brown University, and Rutgers University and received a Ph.D. at Yale University in 1995. He is professor of Russian, English, and Jewish studies at Boston College, where he cofounded the Jewish Studies Program, and an associate at Harvard University's Davis Center, where he directs the seminar on Jews of Russia. Shrayer edits the book series "Jews of Russia & Eastern Europe and Their Legacy" at Academic Studies Press.

Maxim D. Shrayer has authored and edited over ten books of criticism, biography, nonfiction, fiction, poetry, and translation, among them the critical studies *The World of Nabokov's Stories* and *Russian Poet/Soviet*

Jew. He is the author of the acclaimed literary memoirs *Waiting for America: A Story of Emigration* and *Leaving Russia: A Jewish Story* (finalist of the 2013 National Jewish Book Award), of the story collection *Yom Kippur in Amsterdam*, and of three collections of Russian-language poetry. He has also edited and cotranslated three books of fiction by his father, David Shrayer-Petrov, for the Library of Modern Jewish Literature. Shrayer won a 2007 National Jewish Book Award for his two-volume *Anthology of Jewish-Russian Literature*. His book *I Saw It: Ilya Selvinsky and the Legacy of Bearing Witness to the Shoah* appeared in 2013. Shrayer's new book, *Bunin and Nabokov: A History of Rivalry*, was published in 2014 in Moscow and became a national bestseller. Shrayer's works have been translated into eight languages.

Shrayer is the recipient of a number of awards and fellowships, including those from the Guggenheim Foundation, the National Endowment for the Humanities, the Rockefeller Foundation, and the Bogliasco Foundation. He lectures widely on topics ranging from the legacy of the refusenik movement and the experience of ex-Soviet Jews in America to Shoah literature and Jewish-Russian culture. Shrayer lives in Massachusetts with his wife, Dr. Karen E. Lasser, a medical researcher and physician, and their two daughters. They divide their time between Brookline and South Chatham.

For more information, visit Shrayer's website at *www.shrayer.com*.

Praise for Shrayer's *With or Without You*

"Lucid and insightful, Maxim D. Shrayer reminds why so many Russian Jews left the country they once called their own, and explains why those who stayed are still unsure if they belong. Clearly written and very readable."

—Anne Applebaum, *Washington Post* columnist
and author of *Gulag* and *Red Famine*

"An illuminating first-person narrative about the minority of Russian Jews who have remained, against all odds, in their mother country—and also about Russia, a country continuously losing its Jews. At this point, we know more about the refuseniks of the past than about Russia's Jews of the present. Any information about these remaining Jews—a peculiar crowd, vulnerable and powerful at once—is precious. This book does an excellent job in telling their collective and personal stories with the ease and humor of an experienced Jewish storyteller."

—Alexander Etkind, Mikhail M. Bakhtin Professor of History
of Russia-Europe Relations, European University
Institute and author of *Internal Colonization:
Russia's Imperial Experience*

"From the perspective of an émigré who spent his formative years in Moscow, Maxim D. Shrayer reflects on his visit to his native city in 2016. His interviews with several types of Jews and his own acute observations, those of an 'outsider-insider,' yield penetrating insights into the complex situation of Russian Jews today. No longer the objects of overt public antisemitism, their ties to Jewishness are ever more tenuous as their numbers continue to decline rapidly and as they, like many other diaspora Jews, 'integrate' ever more into Russian society."

—Zvi Gitelman, Preston R. Tisch Professor of Judaic Studies,
University of Michigan and author of *A Century of Ambivalence:
The Jews of Russia and the Soviet Union,
1881 to the Present*

"In this concise and clear-headed book Maxim D. Shrayer has managed to convey all the complexity of the present-day condition of Russia's Jewry. Sociological analysis is intertwined with a former refusenik's acute personal observations; youthful memories of Moscow (all émigrés are forever frozen in the age when they left) are superimposed on adult ruminations of a father showing his eleven-year old daughter around his native city. A remarkable investigation, emotionally colored and unerringly precise."

—Luba Jurgenson, Professor,
Université Paris IV-Sorbonne and author
of *Création et Tyrannie: URSS 1917-1991*

"For anyone with an interest in Russian Jewry or post-Soviet Russia this book is a must-read. Wonderfully written, it is full of thought-provoking insights about the past and future of what had once been the largest Jewish community in the world."

—Samuel D. Kassow, Charles H. Northam Professor
of History, Trinity College and author of *Who Will Write Our History: Emanuel Ringelblum and the Oyneg Shabes Archive*

"Did the Creator make a mistake by placing the Jews in the confines of the Russian Empire, asks one of Isaac Babel's characters. Maxim D. Shrayer asks a different question: Did the Creator try to correct this mistake by letting the Jews out of Russia in the course of the last several decades? The answers Shrayer provides in his rich, multi-layered and thought-provoking book put into conversation two different narratives of the Jewish past, one of the Jews who have left, the other of those who have stayed. One cannot grasp the future of the Jews of Russia without reading Maxim D. Shrayer's book."

—Serhii Plokhy, Mykhailo S. Hrushevs'kyi Professor
of Ukrainian History, Harvard University and author
of *Lost Kingdom: The Quest for Empire
and the Making of the Russian Nation*

www.ingramcontent.com/pod-product-compliance
Lightning Source LLC
Chambersburg PA
CBHW070248290326
41930CB00042B/2962